The Fox and the Grapes

An imprint of Om Books International

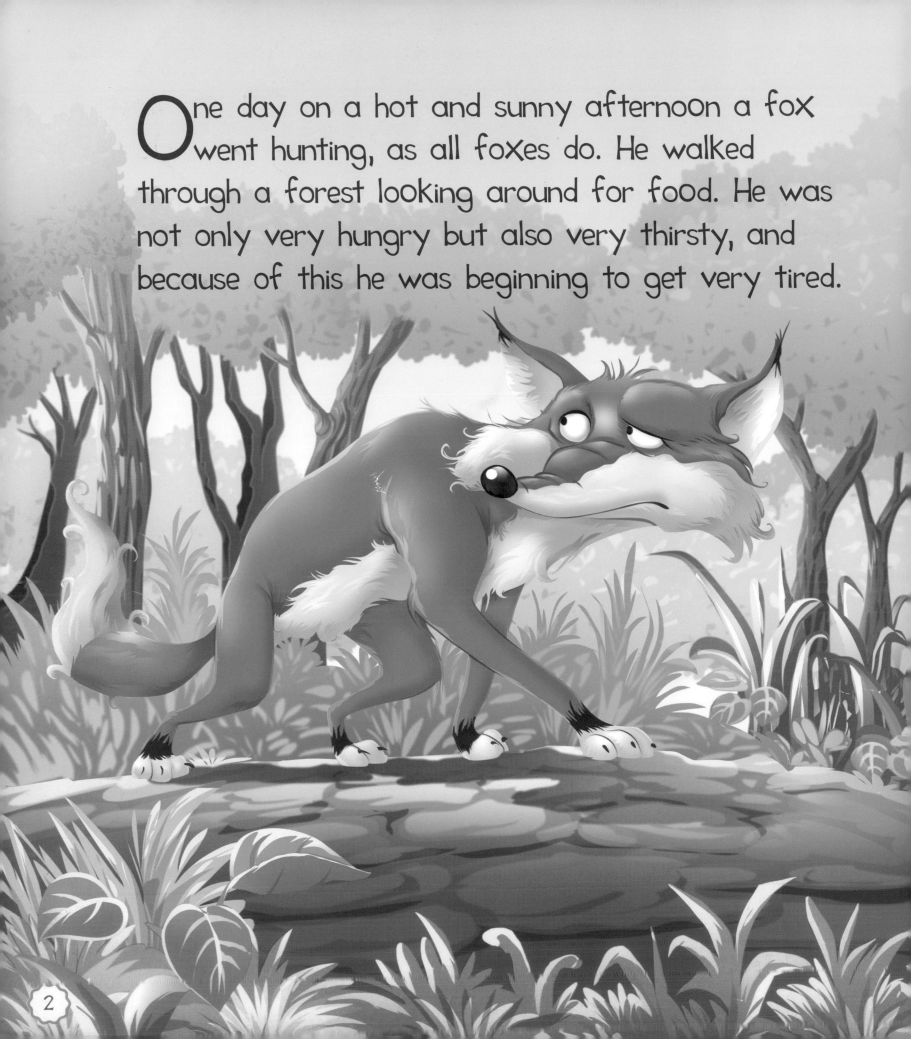

One day on a hot and sunny afternoon a fox went hunting, as all foxes do. He walked through a forest looking around for food. He was not only very hungry but also very thirsty, and because of this he was beginning to get very tired.

He thought to himself, "I have never felt like this in all my life. I wish I could just lie down here and sleep." But he knew that it was important for him to find food. How else would he get his strength back?

Suddenly, just ahead of him, he saw bunches of beautifully ripe, purple grapes. Yummy! His mouth watered as he thought of how juicy and delicious the grapes would be.

He wanted to get his paws into them right away. "What luck," he thought, "just the perfect thing to eat on this hot afternoon."

The grapes were hanging down from a branch just a little above his head.

He went under the lowest bunch and jumped up with his paw stretched out. But he only hit the air. He jumped up again, but could not reach the grapes. They were hanging higher than he could reach.

He went back a few paces to take a run. He thought, "If I run from a distance, I am sure I will be able to jump up higher." He counted, "One, two, three," and ran.

He jumped as high as he could, but missed.
He tried again and again, but it just seemed so
hopeless. All the effort that he was making
seemed to be of no use.

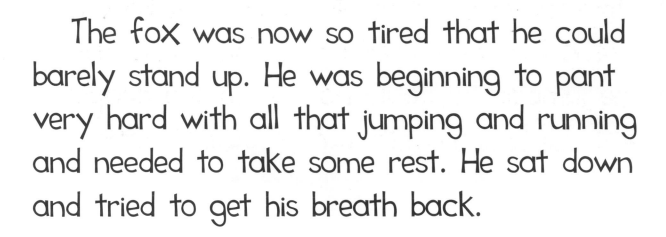

The fox was now so tired that he could barely stand up. He was beginning to pant very hard with all that jumping and running and needed to take some rest. He sat down and tried to get his breath back.

He wanted the grapes so badly that he was willing to try one more time. After a while he felt better. He stood up and tried again. But no matter how high he jumped, he could not reach the grapes. He tried with all his strength, but it did not bring him any luck.

He knew he had to give up! He was not going to get the juicy and delicious purple grapes to eat after all.

This thought made him very angry and disappointed. He was a cunning and smart fox, and he had never had to take defeat like this before.

He began to bark at the grapes. He snarled and showed his teeth.

He said loudly to the grapes, "You horrible sour things, I would not eat you even if you fell off that branch right into my mouth. Who wants to eat sour grapes?"

Then, with a shake of his head, he turned around and walked away with his nose up in the air. As he went he said to himself in a huff, "It does not matter, I would not have enjoyed eating those sour grapes anyway!"

The Fox and the Grapes

On a hot day, a clever fox fails to get his paws on a bunch of juicy grapes hanging from a tree. What will the fox do? Read this story to find out!

Published in 2015 by

An imprint of Om Books International

Corporate & Editorial Office
A-12, Sector 64, Noida 201 301, Uttar Pradesh, India, Phone: +91 120 477 4100
Email: editorial@ombooks.com, Website: www.ombooksinternational.com

Sales Office
107, Ansari Road, Darya Ganj, New Delhi 110 002, India, Phone: +91 11 4000 9000, 2326 3363, 2326 5303
Fax: +91 11 2327 8091, Email: sales@ombooks.com, Website: www.ombooks.com

Copyright © Om Books International 2015

Illustrated by Chandra Prakash Dubey, Madhu Dubey

ISBN: 978-93-84119-69-0

Printed in India

10 9 8 7 6 5 4 3 2 1

Price: ₹ 99

ISBN 978-93-84119-69-0

9 789384 119690

www.ombooksinternational.com